D0487174

Tips for Reading Together

Children learn best when reading is fun.

- Talk about the title and the pictures on the cover.
- Look through the pictures together and discuss what you think the story might be about.
- Read the story together, inviting your child to read as much of it as they can.
- Give lots of praise as your child reads with you, and help them when necessary.
- Try different ways of helping if they get stuck on a word. For example, get them to say the first sound of the word, or break it into chunks, or read the whole sentence again, trying to guess the word. Focus on the meaning.
- Have fun finding the hidden numbers.
- Re-read the story later, encouraging your child to read as much of it as they can.

Children enjoy re-reading stories and this helps to build their confidence.

Have fun!

Find the 10 even numbers hidden in the pictures.

Looking after Gran

Written by Roderick Hunt
Illustrated by Alex Brychta

OXFORD
UNIVERSITY PRESS

The family was going away.

"Look after Floppy," said Dad.

Gran liked looking after Floppy.
She took him for lots of walks.

She threw sticks for him to
chase and balls for him to catch.

Gran had a motorbike.

It was bright red.

"Jump in, Floppy," said Gran.

Gran put on her crash helmet.
"Where are we going?"
thought Floppy.

Soon, they were zooming
into town.

"Isn't this fun!" said Gran.

"Not for me!" thought Floppy.

At last, Gran stopped. She parked
the motorbike on the sand.

"Stay here, Floppy," said Gran.
"Look after the motorbike. I'm
going shopping."

Gran was away for a long time.
The tide started to come in. A wave
splashed the front wheel.

Then a wave splashed the back wheel.

"Gran has parked too close to the sea!" thought Floppy.

"I must find Gran," thought
Floppy.

He ran into the town as fast
as he could.

Sniff! Sniff! went Floppy.
He could tell where Gran
had been. She had been in the
butcher's shop.

"Yum! Bones," thought Floppy.

"Get out!" yelled the butcher. "No dogs in here!"

Floppy ran back into
the street.

"I must find Gran," he
thought.

Sniff! Sniff! went Floppy.

Gran had been in the bread shop.

"Get out!" yelled the baker. "No dogs in here!"

Floppy ran back into
the street.

"I must find Gran,"
he thought.

Then Floppy saw Gran.

She was in the hat shop.

Floppy ran in and barked.

"Get out!" said the lady. "No dogs
in here!"

"Come on, Gran!" thought Floppy.

Floppy ran out of the shop.

Gran ran after him.

"Come back!" called the lady.

"You haven't paid for that hat."

Floppy ran
back to the beach.
Gran puffed
after him.

"Oh no! My motorbike,"
shouted Gran.

She ran into the sea and pushed
her motorbike out.

"Well done, Floppy," said Gran.
"You saved my motorbike!"

Gran spoke to Mum.

"I'm not looking after Floppy," she said. "He's looking after me!"

Think about the story

Why didn't Floppy like going on Gran's motorbike?

Why did Gran leave Floppy with her motorbike?

Gran told Floppy to stay. Why was he right not to stay?

What animal would you like to look after for a day?

Spot the difference

Find the 10 differences on the motorbikes.

Useful common words repeated in this story and other books at Level 4.

after   away   back   been   find   get   going   here   looking
must   my   thought   where

Names in this story: Mum   Dad   Gran   Floppy

More books for you to enjoy

Level 1: Getting Ready	Level 2: Starting to Read	Level 3: Becoming a Reader	Level 4: Building Confidence	Level 5: Reading with Confidence

OXFORD
UNIVERSITY PRESS

Great Clarendon Street,
Oxford OX2 6DP

Text © Roderick Hunt 2005
Illustrations © Alex Brychta 2005
Designed by Andy Wilson

First published 2005
All rights reserved

British Library Cataloguing
in Publication Data available

ISBN 978-0-19-838565-3

10 9 8 7 6 5 4

Printed in China by Imago

Have more fun
with Read at Home